~Lost~ Cornwall

FROM MAGIC LANTERN SLIDES

Jack Ingrey in his office at Shop, St Merryn.

Jack Ingrey, a true Cornishman born in St Merryn in 1915 whom I met late in his life. About 1995 Donald Rawe introduced me to Jack; we clicked right away, being both interested in the same subjects—local history, nature and photography. Jack took me under his wing and I became a very regular visitor along with my two pre-school sons, Chris and Greg. My sons were delighted as Auntie Margaret would take them for a walk to the sweet shop in Shop, St Merryn. Until Jack's untimely death in 2005 we were inseparable despite our age difference. Jack became my best friend and like a second father and second brother rolled into one to me. I miss him dearly and wish to dedicate this book to him and his widow Margaret Ingrey.

~Lost~ Cornwall

FROM MAGIC LANTERN SLIDES

Malcolm McCarthy

Foreword by Rick Stein

FONTHILL

Fonthill Media Limited
Fonthill Media LLC
www.fonthillmedia.com
office@fonthillmedia.com

First published in the United Kingdom
and the United States of America 2016

British Library Cataloguing in Publication Data:
A catalogue record for this book is available from the British Library

ISBN 978-1-78155-290-2

Typeset in 10pt on 13pt Sabon
Printed and bound in Great Britain by TJ International Ltd. Padstow

Foreword

An absolutely fascinating journey in pictures back in time to a remote and far away country that was Cornwall. I think we all share a longing for an innocent past but looking at the slide of Cornish miners deep below or the state of repair of many of the houses it's so clear how incredibly tough life was then. Nevertheless, there is a lyrical pastoral beauty about many of these pictures.

Rick Stein, 2016

A charming busy street scene of Market Street, Falmouth *c.* 1890; be amazed a the clarity and sharpness of this early example of the photographers art.

Acknowledgements

I have been collecting old photographs since 1977, much to my wife Pat's chagrin. She very patiently attended countless postcard fairs and on our holidays back to my family home in Padstow she would patiently accompany me when I would visit older locals to identify people in the photos. This has been going on for many years and I thank her for her saintly patience. I have to thank George Barnes for his help proof reading the Penzance and West Penwith images, putting me straight when I was wrong. Paulette Vanhove also helped greatly with Penzance and Newlyn images. Mark Camp of Looe TIC was a marvel helping with the identification of the Looe area photographs. Tony Brooks has been my man to go to with any mining related questions; he along with his fellow experts Tony Clarke and John Watton have helped me enormously making sure the mining information was correct. Invaluable help providing information for the Boscastle area photos was supplied by the enthusiastic local Sharon Burrell. My mate from Port Isaac Geoff Provis, is a goldmine of information for anything Port Isaac related so I am deeply indebted to him. A very special mention must go to James Plater who has worked marvels repairing, cleaning and enhancing many of the images. I am indebted to him for his skills which have made a huge difference to the quality of the images. He is a professional photograph restorer and I highly recommend his work which can be accessed through his website Cherished Pictures at http://www.cherishedcollection.com/

I would also like to take this opportunity of thanking Brian and Anne Carol for giving me a series of old cine films local to St Merryn, taken by Anne's father John Rossiter. These have been transferred to DVD and are now housed at the County Record Office Truro. Anne also kindly gave me a collection of material by St Merryn photographer Alex Old some of which I will use in the next book.

I have been commissioned to write three books in this series of which this is the first, to be able to complete this task to the best of my ability I needed to identify many photos in my collection which I had not previously researched. This seemed a daunting task until I had a brainwave: set up a Facebook page. This I did and I called it *Unidentified Cornish Photos*. This page proved hugely popular, but even more important it managed to identify 400 unidentified images in the first two weeks.

Any person who was first to identify a photo has been acknowledged with my thanks, so many thanks to the following people: Amelia Bray, Andrew Craze, Andrew Langdon, Angela Blakeway, Barry Swabey, Beverly Morgan, Bonnie Bouckam, Brian

Murrish, Cam Longmuir, Carole Catterall, Catherine May, Cheryl Rail, Chris Walker, Clive Tilley, Darran Barker, Dave Rogers, David Barnicoat, David Thomas, Dawn Phillips, Dee Edwards, Darren Hocking, Diane Donohue, Edwina Hannaford, Elizabeth Carne, Francis Gist, Gemma May, Geoff Provis, George Barnes, Gerry Bloomfield, Giles Thomas, Gordon Fielder, Graham Wood, Heather Lee, Ian Delve, Ian Dudley, Ian Polmear, Ian Valantine, Ian Williams, James Gossop, Jack Trounson, Jane Tutte, Jane Tutle, Janet Axton, Janusz Kowalski, Jaqueline Nowakowski, Jennifer Alsop, Jessica Tamblyn, Jo Bussell, John Bernard, John Brush, John Juleff, John Reade, John Wallis, Jon Pearn, Julie Treneer, Kane Jones, Kay Halley, Len Sheppard, Lesley Andrew, Lesley Taylor, Liam Nankervis, Linda Trevethan, Linda Wilton-Farness, Liz Grant, Liz Hocking, Looe TIC, Lora Winkett, Louise and Nigel Haywood, Luke Chown, Mac Mc Carthy, Maggie Perkins, Malcolm Dyer, Marcus Coad, Mark Camp, Martin Mason, Matthew Stevens, Melanie Huggins, Merv Davey, Meryl Delve, Michael Vian Clark, Mick Franklin, Mike Harcum, Mike Hewitt, Myra Cordingly, Nigel Blake, Pat Miller, Paulette Vanhove, Peter Cogar Pollard, Peter Tonkin, Phil Rodda, Philip Gee, Rachel Bargery Horton, Richard Fletcher, Richard Stevens, Rick Cornwall, Rob Atkinson, Robert Adams, Robert Taylor, Robin Chiffers, Robin Turner, Rodney and Pat Bate, Ross Oliver Collins, Rowan Smith, Sandra Pritchard, Sara Louise Lobb, Sara Penny, Sharon Edwards, Sharon Marie Burrell, Simon Lethlane, Simone Marjelam, Stan Spry, Steve Jeffers, Steve Northcott, Sue Alvey, Sue Dent, Sue Kinver, Sue Nicholas, Sue Vanstone, Suzanne Jane Lawrence, Tamsin Dower, Terry Higman, Tom Murt, Tony Allen, Tony Brooks, Tony Clarke, Tony Johnson, Tracey Dawson, Tracy Childs, Trev Lawrence, Trudie Pearce, Victoria White, Vivien Botterell, Weni Tarling and William John Watton.

Introduction

Being fortunate enough to be born a Cornishman and not realising how incredibly lucky I was until I left the Duchy, every time I returned to my native Padstow on short holidays, staying at my parents, I yearned to come home. The beauty of the estuary and the cornfields, the ever changing landscape dependant on the state of the tide, direction of the wind and cloud cover was something I tried relentlessly to capture on film with poor results. This is why I marvel at the skill of the early photographers who with their primitive equipment managed to frame fantastic moments in time on film.

How we live our lives has changed tremendously in that lifetime-and-a-half. The way we work, dress, live and transport ourselves has changed beyond our forefathers expectations, and how they would marvel at how we live in this day and age. Spare a thought for how hard life was for these souls; if they did not work they did not eat—a far cry from today's welfare system. This book will take you back to a time when Cornwall was inhabited mainly by the Cornish; the Cornish dialect was everywhere and we had our own culture. Sadly those days have gone never to return.

Magic lantern slides have been around as a form of entertainment from the seventeenth century. Since the dawn of photography the potential to put images on glass slides proved technically impossible until the 1880s. Once images were put on glass and projected onto walls and screens all over the world, the potential was soon realised to use lantern slides as teaching aids; for lectures, or just showing the family holiday photographs at the local Church hall.

The size of the slide varied greatly but the vast majority of photographic slides were four inches square; prior to that a variety of sizes were beautifully made in wood with painted glass sporting mechanical workings which animated the slide. The four inch slide became standard.

In this day and age we are so used to putting a 'point and shoot' camera in our pocket— using our smart phone or tablet—that we do not spare a thought for the Victorian and Edwardian photographer who had to carry a large plate camera, a heavy wooden tripod and glass plates for the image to be developed on. Taking photographs at that time was a daunting task; especially when photographers favoured cliff tops or other inaccessible places.

In the years when many of these photographs were taken it was still a steep learning curve for many of these men and the very occasional woman. Taking this into consideration, some of the photographs are remarkably sharp. Some of the better quality and more interesting photographs have been printed full page so the reader may appreciate the detail of the image. I never cease to be amazed by the skill of some of these early photographers. I grew up collecting local images and in particular I have been familiar for many decades with photographer Alex Old.

St Merryn Churchtown where Alex lived was at that time a tiny village that was just becoming popular with the tourist trade. He produced local postcards of startling quality and the two slides of Miss Alchin are his only works in this book.

I do wonder what caused the spark in these people in such small villages. It was not just a case of taking the photograph; they had to have a dark room with all the chemicals to develop print and fix the images, no small or cheap undertaking and a task that definitely required considerable skill.

Slides are generally made from two squares of glass bound together by tape on the outside. Between the two pieces of glass there is normally a black paper mount used to frame the image so that when projected it gives the image a truly professional finish. One piece of glass has the emulsion on; the other is just plain glass to protect the emulsion. Being glass they are prone to cracking. If it is the glass with the emulsion on that has cracked there is little that can be done, but if the crack is on the plain piece of glass, then with care the slide can be dismantled and the plain glass replaced. Unfortunately, like falling buttered bread, nine times out of ten the glass with the crack is the piece with the emulsion on.

Rarely slides are coloured. Those before the 1940s are hand coloured, but later on some slides were made by using colour film. After the early 1950s glass slides went out of fashion as smaller 35 mm cameras held slide film, and the new 35 mm film transparency replaced the glass magic lantern slide. Some of the slides used in this book are coloured but unfortunately being a mono book they are printed in black and white.

All the underground mining slides and some of the above ground mining photographs were taken by J. C. Burrow FRPS who in 1893 printed a book called *Mongst Mines and Miners Underground*, being a series of images and a brief description of how he took them. Burrow was a true pioneer and is one of Cornwall's unsung heroes. Of the one hundred plates he took for this book he only considered twenty-four to be of sufficient quality to be used. The difficulties he faced can best be portrayed by quoting the following passage from this excellent work:

> After preliminary trials with camera varying in size from 10 × 8 to half plate, it was finally determined to use the later because of its lightness, portability and moderate size, the latter being specifically important in confined situations. The light bellows Kinnear form of camera was most suitable. Double dark slides were used carrying fourteen plates, but such were the difficulties experienced that often five or six plates only could be exposed on the same day. When changing plates underground there was no danger of their being damaged by the light, for when the candles were extinguished there was absolute darkness. But, since it was impossible to keep one's hands clean underground, it was found better to take the plates well protected in dark slides. Lenses of all descriptions were tried, with more or less success. The rapid symmetrical did very well for certain subjects, and a half-plate portrait combination was fairly good when used in open place where the subject did not require great depth of focus. Care was, of course, taken to prevent flare spot. The ordinary wide angle was much too slow. A lens having all the advantages of each of these was required, one that would embrace a

wide angle, give depth of focus, and speed. This was found to be Zeiss' Anastigmat, Series III, made by Messrs Ross & Co. It proved to be a perfect gem, and with it splendid results have been obtained, both underground and at surface. A sliding tripod stand was most convenient. Sometimes the camera had to be tilted at an angle of 60° and the front leg tied to rock to prevent overbalancing. At other times it was strapped to a ladder, or a bar, looking down an inclined shaft, or fixed on the ends of a couple of stout planks over a yawning "gunnies." The sliding form of a tripod allowed the greatest freedom in such situations.

The best apparatus manufactured is of no practical value without good plates. On this subject, so important to the photographer, pages might be written with the experiences of a twelvemonth underground. The plates of several makers were tried, slow plates, rapid plates and isochromatic plates. But none equalled the Cadett lighting plate. At first all the candles were extinguished, as the halo round each spoiled the effect of the picture, but, with the lightning plate, every miner was taken in his working position, with his light in its usual place. So sensitive were these plates that the camera had to be well covered to prevent any stray pencil of light being admitted other than through the lens. This requires careful attention when working in daylight. The diaphragm slit in the lens, even, should be covered, say, by means of a wide india-rubber band.

It is needless to detail the incidents attending the transport of apparatus from surface to the bottom of an inclined shaft half-a-mile below. Some were unpleasant, many were amusing. Occasionally the band of willing helpers were recruited from certain classes of individuals totally unaccustomed to mining and mines. Readers intending to attempt underground photography must not be discouraged when a too eager assistant, staggering through the semi-darkness with a hydrogen cylinder of 20 feet capacity under his arm, and a pair of lime-light burners in one hand, stumbles headlong into a pool of water by the side of the level. Nor must they lose their self-control when, after carefully selecting the driest spot available to open the magnesium powder tin for re-charging the lamps, a "flosh" of water from some unknown source falls into the tin as soon as the cover is off, instantly "dropping the curtain" most effectually upon the remainder of the day's programme. The temptation to place on record many incidents, annoying at the time of occurrence, but extremely interesting as reminiscences, become strong. On one occasion, just as arrangements for a first shot of the camera were completed, a strong voice, some ten fathoms overhead shouted, "Hallo, down there. Fire" "Don't fire yet," was the reply "We have fired. Go back under the stull." To late to postpone matters, the only thing left to do was to ask "How many?" "Three. Look out" In a few moments, bang, bang, bang, went three holes, the roar of falling stuff followed, and a few loose stones rattled down the foot-wall to the place where the camera had been fixed. This meant waiting for the atmosphere to regain sufficient degree of clearness, and, of course, re-fixing the whole of the apparatus.

The preparations required were more extensive than one imagines. Each helper undertook a particular duty. One adjusted the lime-light burners, another attended the oxygen and hydrogen cylinders and trappings, another prepared the magnesium lamps, and so on. The writer, after repeated unsatisfactory experiments with different flash-lamps, designed a pair of triple-flash lamps, which have proved exceedingly useful and have given most satisfactory results. The high temperatures of the deep mines caused camera and lens to be covered with condensed vapour for some time after the scene of operations was reached, a source of much bother.

Above: This incredible photo by J. C. Burrows is taken at the bottom of the engine shaft in Cooks Kitchen Mine in Pool. This is the bottom of the pumping system with a short bucket lift raising water up to the next level whence it was pumped to surface. This bucket lift would have been connected to the main pump rod operated by the pumping engine on the surface and used to pump water out of the shaft. On the left two miners are working a rock drill.

Opposite: Lansallos Street, Polperro looking towards the Harbour. An old fisherman sits in the sun with a toddler on his lap beside the Jews House.

A state of readiness having been arrived at, the word to "light up" produced a powerful flash from the lamps and ribbons simultaneously. The lime-lights were previously at their maximum intensity. An exposure of from two to four seconds generally gave the best results. If everything appeared favourable in the strong light, another subject was sought; for a second exposure, in the same place, on the same day, rarely gave good results owing to the "fog" caused by the products of the combustion of the magnesium. For close subjects triple-flash magnesium lamps were generally used, so placed as to destroy shadow as much as possible, but in large areas, such as that shown in Dolcoath Man Engine more lamps were brought into requisition. In such areas the air was generally cooler and clearer, and sometimes two exposures in succession gave fair results under such circumstances. The bottom of the shaft in Cook's Kitchen Mine was a difficult subject. The temperature there was 100 degrees F. The miners work nearly naked. The camera was attached to the ladder and tilted to an angle of 45 degrees. Water dropped everywhere and came down from the foot-wall in a steady stream. Heat water and vapour, combine with the peculiar setting of the camera, made the work tedious and difficult...

The next time you 'point and shoot' have a thought for those early photographers whose work we take for granted with just a glance. When you look at their work think about the arduous journey and difficulty setting up the shot, and the expense involved.

Occasionally the reader may find a few words which are unfamiliar to you if you are not born and bred Cornish. 'Maun' is a wicker basket; 'withy' is the material used to make crab pots, normally young willow shoots. 'Croust' is a mid-morning meal; 'drang' is a narrow alleyway and 'gramfer' is pretty obviously grandfather. I Hope this helps.

I would like to finish by saying that without the help of the many people mentioned in the acknowledgments this book would not have been possible. Every effort has been made to ensure the information is correct but there are bound to be mistakes. My name is on the cover but if I could have I would have put everyone in the acknowledgements name on it, thank you all so much.

I hope that you enjoy this book, with all the images being selected from my personal collection. If you have any questions please feel free to email me.

Malcolm McCarthy
taclowcoth@aol.com
Padstow, July 2015

A rustic scene of Stratton looking from Binhamy Hill, Stratton church is prominent in the distance. Stratton lies close to Bude and two miles east of the north Cornish coast.

Left: Stratton's old prison door, it was found in the porch of St Andrews church Stratton. The door has CLINK written in hobnails. The word clink originates from the prison on the north side of the River Thames called the Clink.

Below: The historic Tree Inn located in Fore Street Stratton. The Tree Inn was formerly the manor house. Anthony Payne the Cornish giant measuring seven foot four inches was born in the house in 1612.

This photo is of the bottom of the Coombe Valley which is dissected by a meandering stream running down the valley to emerge onto the beach at Duckpond. Coombe is in the parish of Morwenstow.

A photo taken in the 1900s of a quaint thatched cottage in Kilkhampton village. The cottage used to stand on the A39 next to the present day post office.

Above: Barnstaple registered but Bude-owned *Traly*, a steel west-country trading ketch moored up in Bude canal. She came to Bude in 1936 and worked from the port until 1958 when she was sold to the Baltic trade. She was built for the Irish trade in 1912.

Below: An incredible image probably by Bude photographer H. Thorne, looking from Bude Haven towards the entrance to Bude Canal. Bude Canal was originally built to transport the mineral-rich sand from Bude Haven inland, to the agricultural lands to dress the fields. Tub boats were used to transport the sand along the canal. The canal which was 35 miles long and rose from sea level to an altitude of 443 feet, it was opened on 8 July 1823 at a cost of £118,000.

C. 1900, an unknown field in North Cornwall. A field hand or farmer sharpens the cutting blades of the hay cutting machine, a wooden hay rake lies beside his straw-work basket.

Above: Inside Morwenstow parish church looking at the twelfth century arches illustrating the wonderful decorative Norman carving. The church of St Morwenna and St John the Baptist is the parish church of Morwenstow, and the most northerly church in Cornwall. The present Norman church was built on the site of an earlier Saxon church, though most of the present structure dates from the thirteenth to sixteenth centuries. Morwenstow is famous for the Victorian author and antiquarian Reverend Robert Stephen Hawker who was vicar of the parish.

Below: Crackington Haven a view from Pentreath Hill looking seaward towards the Haven, the property first left is called Pentreath. The building with the whitish roof to the left was the linhay or calves house belonging to Crackington Manor which is the 'L'-shaped building in the centre of the cluster. To the right of the manor house is Manor Cottage. High on the headland on the left is Tremoutha Farm. The two headlands seawards of the Haven beach and Tremoutha Orm are called Big Cam and Little Cam.

Above: The congregation parade into Minster Church in the Valency Valley, Boscastle. Minster church is built on the site of an old monastery, the monks who inhabited the monastery were tailors and this is commemorated by a granite stone with a pair of scissors carved into it and set in to the tower wall.

Below: Looking up Boscastle High Street in1904. The large house on the right is Hildene House run as a guest house by the Nicholls family; above that Hildene Cottage, Mr Hancock lived in the house above the cottage. Behind Hildene House was a dairy which was later run by Mrs Eliza Nicholls. Opposite with the gaggle of people outside was St Christopher's Hotel.

Above: Taken in 1904, this early Edwardian slide is looking down Fore Street, Boscastle, towards Dunn Street.

Below: Another Edwardian slide taken in Boscastle, taken on the same day in 1904 as the previous two images. This time the photographer is looking up Fore Street towards the High Street. The building on the right above the telegraph pole is Boscastle School; next door to the school is Tinkers cottage. Top right of the street above the telegraph pole is the Napoleon Inn; Boscastle's oldest pub.

Above: Tinkers Cottage in Fore Street Boscastle. It is said there were smugglers tunnels that run under these cottages right down to the harbour. Tinkers cottage and its neighbours are near Boscastle old castle site, probably amongst the oldest houses in the village.

Below: Boscastle Bridge *c.* 1900; it was situated at the bottom of the village near the harbour. This bridge was rebuilt in the late 1950s due to flood damage and road widening.

Above: An Edwardian photo of a lady strolling along Boscastle harbour wall; she is looking down at the entrance to the harbour. The protruding rock on the cliff is called the Queens Head. Cork net floats and a mast and ruinous withy crab pots adorn the harbour wall.

Below: An Edwardian view of Boscastle harbour, showing the breakwater which was built to protect vessels against the North Cornish coast's aggressive ground sea and run. Boscastle fishing vessels are registered with the Padstow or PW registration.

Rocky Valley is a very beautiful and holy place. It is home to the medieval whitewashed chapel of St Piran. St Piran's Well, a slate beehive structure with an iron cross atop it stands beside the lane that runs past the Rocky Valley Hotel. Further down the valley is the hermitage of St Nectan. The valley has been cut to a depth from top to bottom of 75 feet by the action of the Trevillet River.

The fifteenth century Trevillet Mill is situated in the Rocky Valley, Trethevy near Bossiney which is between Boscastle and Tintagel. Trevillet Mill was made famous by Thomas Creswick in 1851 featuring in his painting *The Valley Mill*.

Above: St Nectan's Knieve is situated in St Nectan's Glen Trethevy in the Rocky Valley. This Edwardian photo shows the stream entering the plunge pool at the bottom of the twenty metre waterfall. Its name is derived from the hermit St Nectan. Unsubstantiated legend has it that he lived in a cell above the waterfall. As you walk down the valley ancient curious serpentine carvings are visible in the slate; this has been a holy and special site for a very long time.

Below: A view from Island Courtyard into the centre of Tintagel Castle looking across at the medieval Lower Mainland Courtyard, the original entrance to the castle.

Above: An Edwardian slide looking down the Vale of Avalon known locally as Castle Path, Tintagel. This path leads to the beach and Merlin's Cave below the castle ruins, the castle can be seen on the top of the hill on the left. The derelict building on the left hand side of the road is the remains of an old mill; the rock overhang on the right hand side was removed in the 1920s.

Right: The beach which for many years was a harbour, where sailing ships would bring goods in to the castle site. The old winch used for lifting cargo from the beach to the walkway can clearly be seen. The winch was also used to lift small craft to the safety of the rock platform. Merlin's Cave can be seen in the cliff on the right of the photo and above on the cliff top are the walls of the castle.

Above: A view through the medieval walls of the Island Courtyard in Tintagel's famous castle, looking out through the castle walls over the Atlantic Ocean. The castle covers a vast and rugged area of the north Cornish cliffs, and in its day must have been a daunting sight.

Below: A charming slide of an Edwardian lady pictured sketching the Old Post Office, Tintagel. The herringbone wall in front of the post office was a modern addition at the time the photo was taken as earlier photos show no wall at all at this point. The building was originally a fourteenth century yeoman farmer's house. It is probably one of the most photographed buildings in the Duchy with its distinctive undulating roof and huge chimney stack. The building was acquired by the National Trust in 1903, about the time this photograph was taken.

Above: The Old Toll House, one of Tintagel's ancient houses, situated on the Bossiney Road; the B 3263 which is the main Road from Tintagel to Boscastle. This lonely cottage is now unbelievably in a terrace of buildings in the middle of the village, now trading as the Cottage Tea Rooms.

Below: The coffin rest at Tintagel's eleventh century Parish Church of St Mareriana. In 1888 a roman milestone that was being used as a coffin rest was moved inside the church for safety. The milestone commemorated Emperor Galerius Valerius Licinianus. The inscription reads: IMPCG VAL LICIN.

Above: Port Gavern is a small hamlet near Port Isaac. In its hey-day, it was a busy little port exporting slate from the Delabole slate quarry, and importing coal. The cargoes were unloaded directly on to wagons from the ships as there were no wharves or piers. The arrival of the railway to Wadebridge was the death knell of Port Gavern as the slate was thereafter transported by rail. Here two fishermen are working on the mast of one of the half a dozen small luggers on the beach.

Below: The Town Platt at Port Isaac *c.* 1900. The Platt situated at the top of the beach was later concreted over. This area was used as a small public area; fairs were held on the Platt in the olden days, and it was also used to lay-up boats when required. At the time this photo was taken the boats were hauled by hand up the beach, later a winch was fitted where the large white stone is located. The street on the right is Fore Street, and the building with large doors has had various uses over the years from inns to shops.

A small shop at the bottom of Port Isaac, the fish cellars are on the right.

Church Hill Port Isaac. On the left was Tremain's shop which sold almost anything. First on the right was Worden's butcher's shop, and the second shop on the right was Hawken's shop which was a general stores, being a chandlery, grocery and drapery retailer.

This slide shows the bottom of Dolphin Street Port Isaac. The sign on the left advertises the Dolphin Inn. The large sign on the right is a Great Western Railway advertisement. The bottom of the building with the large sign on was used as a bark house for barking nets, later the top floor was used as the dole office. At the time of writing this, of the thirty-six cottages in Dolphin Street most are holiday cottages; a sad sign of the times.

Middle Street Port Isaac; the rear of Slipway House at the leat. The leat is known by Port Isaac folk as the Lake. For information, Newlyn folk also call a leat a lake—something I was unfamiliar with until researching this book.

Right: An Edwardian slide of Temple Bar, Port Isaac; a narrow lane connecting Fore Street with Dolphin Street. This alleyway was once in the Guinness Book of Records as being the narrowest in the world. In the 1950s it was locally known as Squeeze Belly Alley.

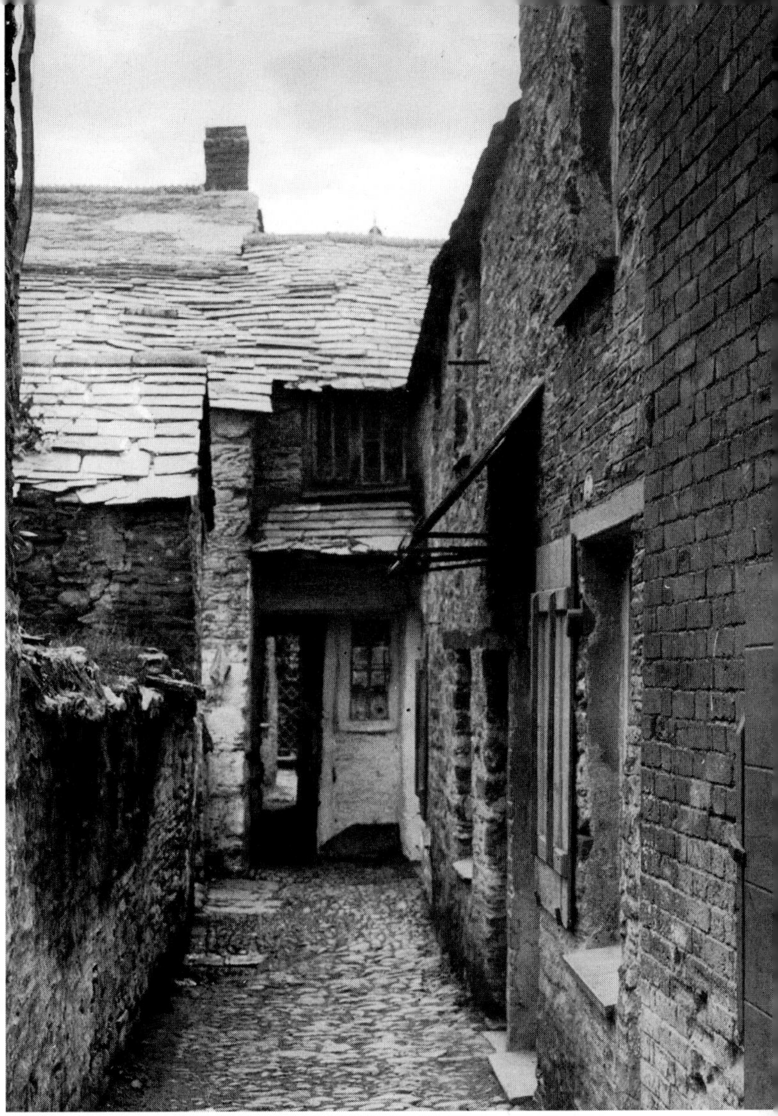

Below: An early twentieth century image of Pentus and the Pentus Fish Cellars. The photo is taken from Port Isaac beach. Behind the low cellars can be seen the houses in Fore Street.

Port Isaac Beach looking up towards the village. Boats are pulled up out of the water onto the Platt above the strand line. Fore Street runs off to the left in the shadows

A young Edwardian girl eats her pasty on a large rock surrounded by shingle at the top of Port Isaac beach. She is surrounded by fishing detritus; sails drying, an old wicker maun, withy pots and fishing boats pulled up on to the Platt.

Carts and carriages on Port Isaac beach beside a group of fishermen gathered around a small lugger at low tide. In this photo the cove is open to the elements. A breakwater now protects this small harbour from the violent actions of the Atlantic Ocean.

The local Port Isaac luggers have returned from fishing; two are pulled up on the beach awaiting the next flood tide while others are at anchor.

Left: A charming photo *c.* 1900 of two old lime-washed cottages, the gardens built above the cliffs just below the school in Fore Street, Port Isaac.

Below: A later view of Port Isaac. Some of the fishing fleet are at their moorings, the remainder are pulled up on to the beach. This slide shows beautifully how the town has been built around the beach and then spread back up the valley.

Church Hill, Port Isaac looking out over the village. In the distance a lugger can be seen with lug sail out, and far right is the Board school. At the bottom of the hill Tremain's shop sign is visible.

An Edwardian boy moves his pig at Tresarrow, a hamlet near Trelights in St Endellion. The area recently became famous because David Cameron's fourth child Florence Rose Endellion Cameron was named after the parish.

This is a slide of the famous Daniel Gumb's Cave in Stowe Quarry at Minions on Bodmin Moor. In the background can be seen the Cheeswring, a natural structure weathered to this shape over the centuries. Bodmin Moor is both wild and bleak but a beautiful place to visit.

St Cleer is situated on the south-west flank of Bodmin Moor; the ancient St Cleer's Well lies below a fifteenth century structure which covers the well as seen in this Edwardian slide. The cover was built so that the well could be used as a bowssening pool which was used for curing the insane or deranged by total immersion in the holy water.

Sinkinney Church or properly known as St Enodoc Church. Trebetherick, in St Minver parish is a chapel of ease. The church dating from the twelfth Century was buried to roof level from the sixteenth to nineteenth centuries with wind-blown sea sand from the adjacent beach. To be entitled to collect tithes the church had to hold at least one service a year, and access was gained through the roof. The church is no longer buried and is in a beautiful position overlooking the stunning Camel Estuary.

Mr Faull, Padstow's Wesleyan Chapel's blind organist is seen talking to the Padstow Methodist minister outsides Mr Faull's house on North Quay Padstow. The Elizabethan building is unchanged to this day and now trades as an Estate Agency.

Above: One of a pair of slides of a brig being towed into Padstow to unload corn, here she is being towed in by a small steam tug called the *Princess May* past a dredger at work clearing the channel of sand.

Below: In the Dock at Padstow, a crew of men are unloading the corn from the brig seen in the above image. On the tracks a railway wagon houses a steam winch; the rope can be seen running up to the tackle lifting the sacks of corn onto the waiting wagons. Padstow was a very busy port having the advantage of the railway station and fish market right beside the dock. The railway lines ran out along the Dock and also along to the Inner Quay to the China Clay berth.

A beautiful photograph of the *Rhoda Mary*; she is undergoing repairs against the North Quay, Padstow. She was built at Point in Feock by John Stephens in 1868. In 1898 she was changed from a two-masted to a three-masted schooner. In 1908 she was bought by W. S. Allport and worked out of Padstow. This photo would have been taken shortly after she was brought to Padstow.

Above: The Strand Padstow *c.* 1900, the tide is out. These days there is a tidal gate and the water is only let out for repairs or inspection once a year in November. The house Mr Faull can be seen outside of on page 37 can be seen centre of picture. The Strand is unrecognisable today with not one of the walls or buildings remaining.

Opposite above: This slide of the famous Padstow Obby Oss in Clemow's Yard was taken by Padstonian Edward Edyvane. The gates behind the 'oss' led onto the Market which the Peace Oss danced out through to perform its annual perambulation around the town. One of Padstow's two obby oss's it was renamed after the First World War to Peace Oss from its original name, Blue Ribbon Oss, named after the temperance movement which was strong in Padstow in the 1870s. The followers of this 'oss' still wear the blue ribbon to this day whilst the Old Oss sports a red ribbon. The teaser wearing a mask, blue and white bow tie and tails is Mr Bill Thomas. This is the largest slide I have seen being half plate. I have had to crop the bottom due to severe damage to the emulsion sustained after being discarded in the photographer's garden in Barry's Lane Padstow for many years.

Below: This slide which at first glance appears quite ordinary is remarkable when one considers that the lady and photographer have had to climb down an almost vertical 50 foot high cliff which has no path in order to take this picture. It shows the striking stratified cliff formation known as Marble Cliffs which is visible here just east of Trevone. Apparently this rock formation next re-emerges in Germany.

Above and left: Mary Alchin, an eccentric lady who lived in Trevone. She had a very small cottage just above the beach where Pentonwarra now stands. She apparently had a love for animals and was always feeding the birds. Mary was made famous by a postcard by St Merryn photographer Alex Old entitled *A Cornish Beauty* where she is seen gurning. Her brother was a physician to Queen Victoria. These two slides show her in the photograph entitled *A Cornish Beauty* and posing with her great dane.

The old foghorn and compressor house at Trevose Head Lighthouse. The lighthouse, built in 1845, had this horn installed in 1913. Almost 100 years after this photo was taken Trinity House decided, in May 2012, with the automation of lighthouses and modern navigation aids, the foghorn at Trevose was no longer a necessity and it was removed. I live in Padstow about three miles away and it was a familiar sound to me as a child being clearly audible.

The thirteenth-century parish church of St Mawgan; the upper part of the tower and the south isle are a fifteenth century addition to the original cruciform building. The church is dedicated to St Magnus and St Nicholas.

Above: A pre-1892 slide looking across Tolcarne Beach Newquay towards the harbour. The vehicles on the beach are horse-drawn bathing huts.

Left: A charming slide of a Victorian girl practising her golf swing on Tolcarne Beach, Newquay. Beach tents are in evidence under the cliffs in the background.

Two warships anchored in Newquay Bay, they arrived on Tuesday 23 June 1914 staying for a couple of days fundraising for the Great War. HMS *Orion* and HMS *Monarch* were sister ships to HMS *Conqueror* and HMS *Thunderer* which visited Padstow at the same time. Their class were known as super dreadnoughts. Apparently there was an accident on the *Monarch* and three ratings died, two of whom were buried in Newquay.

A general view of Newquay harbour. A ketch is laying alongside the central railway berth; a railway wagon is above her on the quay and it appears that she is using shutes to load china clay.

Above: This lovely slide of Fore Street, Newquay, *c.* 1915 captures a bustling scene. The building on the right was Jenkin & Sons store. If you look at these shops closely today they are remarkable for their original shop fronts and beautiful window detail.

Opposite above and below: St Columb carnival in the 1940s; the carnival is marching down Fair Street towards Fore Street. There is also a close up of the Red Cross float that was in this parade.

Above: St Piran's church Perranzabuloe, this church at the hamlet of Perranzabuloe was rebuilt mainly from the remains of the old church in 1805.

Opposite above and below: St Piran's oratory which was buried beneath Penhale Sands Perranzabuloe. Legend has it that it was built by St Piran on his arrival on Perran Beach from Ireland. The original building is believed to have been wattle and daub but was soon replaced by the stone building. The building was excavated from the sands in 1910 when these two photos were taken, one shows the oratory with two ladies looking at it, the other shows the Cornish historian Thurston Peters addressing the meeting about the oratory. A concrete structure was built around the oratory to protect it after the 1910 excavation. The roof of this was taken off in 1980 and further excavation is being carried out from 2014 onwards. The oratory has its own Facebook page if you would like up to date information.

Above: The wreck of the St Ives lifeboat RNLB *John and Sarah Eliza Stych*. She was on loan from Padstow after the RNLB *Caroline Parsons* was wrecked on service in January 1938 going to the aid of the SS *Alba*. The *Stych* was launched on 22 January 1939 to aid the SS *Wilston* in trouble off Cape Cornwall in mountainous seas. Unfortunately the *Stych* fouled her propeller and was rendered helpless, the tragic result being she was eventually wrecked on Godrevy Point, seven of her eight crew perished: Captain Thomas Cocking, Matthew S. Barber, William B. Barber, John Thomas, Richard D. Stevens, John B. Cocking and Edgar Bassett all sadly lost their lives whilst trying to save others. The sole survivor was William Freeman who managed to scramble up the rocks; all eight crew members were awarded the RNLI's bronze medal. The photo shows the hulk of the lifeboat on Godrevy Point, the extensive damage can clearly be seen; the wreck was later set afire.

Below: This slide entitled *A Cornish Haul* shows a catch of herring or pilchards in one of the Cornish seine boats. From the size of her I would suggest a St Ives or Newlyn vessel. The pilchards would have been packed into barrels with the noses facing the centre in a wheel effect. In Cornwall we would pronounce Herring as 'errin.

Above: A 1920s slide of the Wharf, St Ives and beach front buildings.

Right: A nice street scene showing the Golden Lion Inn, St Ives and the fifteenth century church of St Ives. Pre-1826 the church was a chapel of ease before becoming the parish church, being dedicated to Saint la the Virgin alias St Ives. The four stage granite tower is over eighty feet high.

A charming image of Bailey's Court one of St Ives backstreets *c.* 1910. Well turned out children lounge around in the sun, one holding a miniature maun, another standing in the shade with his hoop and pusher. Washing as always in St Ives is hanging drying and a couple of old wheel barrows complete the idyllic scene.

Above: A wonderfully atmospheric slide of the Digey, St Ives. Two boys ride a donkey cart along the Digey past two ladies wearing their shawls with their washing drying behind them.

Right: Another slide of the Digey, St Ives. This view is not quite as busy as the last, but it still conveys the quaintness of the St Ives cobbled narrow streets.

Bunkers Hill, St Ives. A young girl sits on the boot smoothed steps whilst the washing adorns the cobbled street like a row of bunting; a granite drainage trough runs down the centre of the street.

Skinning dogfish on the beach at St Ives. Note the hand barrows that were used instead of wheel barrows as they are of no use on a pebbly beach. Horse and carts in the background are being used to pull the catch from the off-loading fishing boats.

The top of the slipway at St Ives harbour. Ben Phillips is pictured leaning on the horse; John F. Tomanis seen at the rear of the cart and in the foreground is Tommy Humphries. On the floor are cod and in the maun are turbot.

This 1940's slide is of Bethesda Street, St Ives. Bethesda House on the left became a house in 1918 when Richard and Alice Veal bought the first floor loft and converted it. One of the Veal girls is out in the street in a below knee coat. The little girl on the right is two-year-old Meryl Delve on her grandfather's front step. Smeaton's Tower is visible on the harbour breakwater in the background.

This is of technical interest as it is half of a tiny stereoscopic glass slide. It is a view taken in 1931 of the Lambeth Walk on St Ives seafront, looking towards the Warren. The buildings off to the side are between Westcott's Quay and Pendolva Rocks.

St Ives harbour from above the bus station. The Parish Church of St Ia is evident on the left of the picture; Lambeth Walk is on the left and the harbour front on the right-hand side past the pier wall.

A general view of St Ives looking across at the island and harbour from Hain Walk. Porthminster Beach is the first beach on the left. The right-hand pier is Smeaton's Pier and to the right of this is a small beach called Bamaluz beach.

An atmospheric image of Smeaton's Pier St Ives. A group of fishermen chat on the pier while another kneels as he repairs withy pots.

Above: Rowland's Palace of Variety. This was a travelling showman's attraction and this slide shows it working in Redruth in the early 1900s. The Rowland family are still travelling to this day, being seven generations in the fairground business. They travel the county going to and from various festivals and customs.

Left: Children line up to pose for the camera in Fore Street Camborne in front of the poster-festooned ruinous walls.

Above: This slide captures a piece of Hayle history; the launching of the Hayle lifeboat. She is being launched from a horse drawn carriage. Hayle had a lifeboat on service from 1866, the first boat being provided by Oxford University and named RNLB *Isis*; she was replaced in November 1887 by RNLB *F. H. Harrison*. These first two boats were 32-foot self-righters, the final vessel a 36-foot self-righter was named the *Admiral Rodd*. She was only called to service three times before the station closed in 1907. I am not sure which boat is in the photo but believe it to be one of the latter two boats.

Below: The Men an Toll, three curious standing stones believed to date from the Neolithic era are on the side of the Madron to Morvah road. We know from earlier scholarly plans of the site that the stones have been repositioned and it is believed they could be part of a stone circle. As with curious stones several local superstitions abound, one that on a full moon if a woman passes backwards through the hole that she will become pregnant. Another folk tale is that the stone can cure rickets, and naked children were passed through the hole seven times to cure them of the disease.

Zennor Churchtown. Churchtown is a common suffix in Cornwall and it simply denotes the part of a village that grew around the church. This slide is a charming composition of Edwardian children on the wall in the village with a cluster of buildings in the background surrounding the church.

Back-breaking work is being undertaken in the fields at Carnyorth, Pendeen in this slide. The house in the background is called Atlantic View and it is at the top of the present day Carnyorth Terrace. When this photo was taken Carnyorth Terrace had not been built, the wall in the foreground is still in situ.

The wreck of the 97.5 metre-long steel cargo vessel SS *William Cory.* She ran aground on the rocks at Pendeen on September 1910, just a year after her launch.

This slide shows thatched cottages and the rugged Cape Cornwall landscape at Sennen. Sennen Cove is a very small village with a population of just two hundred people. The village used to be a thriving fishing cove with large catches of mullet being normal. Along with most other villages on the Cornish coast, Sennen now relies mainly on the tourist industry.

Above: Market Square, St Just *c.* 1900. The building on the left is the Kings Arms, and the fifteenth century St Just parish church can be seen on the right hand side of the image. The church is built of granite blocks with limestone pillars and houses two medieval heavily-restored wall paintings; one depicting St George, the other a warning to breakers of the Sabbath.

Left: The wreck of the 87 metre steel cargo vessel SS *J. Duncan* on the rocks at Cape Cornwall. She was built in 1905 in Scotland by Ailsa Shipbuilding for J. T. Duncan and Co. of Cardiff. She ran aground on 14 August 1913.

This little cottage is famed throughout the land as the first and last refreshment house in England. In the early days when this photograph was taken refreshments were provided and small souvenirs sold from this tiny cottage. This refreshment house was started in the mid-nineteenth century by Grace Thomas.

The wreck of the 100 metre-long steel cargo ship SS *City of Cardiff*. She was built by Ropner and Sons Ltd of Stockton on Tees, for Sir William Reardon Smith & Sons in 1906. She was wrecked during a storm on the rocks at Nanjizel near Land's End, 21 March 1912.

Above: The Longships Lighthouse stands about one and a quarter miles off Land's End. The present lighthouse built in 1869 replaced Samuel Wyatt's lighthouse built in 1795. The present building unmanned and fully automated since 1988 has a beam that can be seen at a distant of 11 nautical miles emitting one long flash every five seconds.

Below: Boys are busy picking the sweet-scented narcissi on the Isles of Scilly in the late 1890s. The overseer certainly looks like a stern taskmaster and I am sure he got his money's worth out of the young workers.

It is difficult to capture the wonder of Augustus Smith's sub-tropical Tresco Abbey Gardens created by building tall wind-breaks. The plants have to be seen and smelt to fully appreciate their wonder within a network of small enclosures built around the old priory ruins.

An early view of the Valhalla ships figurehead collection. One can see from this photograph that the building on Tresco is adorned with ships figureheads and carved ships timbers. These high-relief, lifelike garishly painted carvings adorning the building making one wonder at the depth of skill of so many craftsmen in Britain's shipyards of the nineteenth century.

The hulk of the wreck of the Norwegian bark *Sophie of Frederikstad* which had been carrying anthracite from Swansea. On 15 December 1896 she was seen wallowing and dis-masted in heavy seas. When she was boarded the table was laid for a meal but the crew were not on board. She was towed to New Grimsby Tresco; her hulk was sold to Algernon Dorrien-Smith who used the coal to fuel his greenhouses and timbers around his Tresco estate. Behind the wreck are Plumb Rocks, Bryher is on the right and in the far distance is St Mary's.

Opposite above and below: St Buryan Churchtown is near Lands' End and five miles west of Penzance. Its name is derived from the Irish Saint Buriana. The top slide shows St Buryan Churchtown cross; the bottom photograph is of the Churchyard cross. The building on the left in the top photo is the eastern corner of Belmont House, formerly the Kings Arms. To the right is the tower of the Church of St Buryan; the tower having been built in 1501.

ALSO

Above: Lamorna, a small fishing village and cove in Penwith lies nestled in a valley that is protected within Cornwall's Area of Outstanding Beauty. The cove was made famous by the Newlyn School of art and the Lamorna Colony who at the turn of the twentieth century favoured the cove for its light and beauty.

Below: The entrance to Paul churchyard. Paul is famous as Dolly Pentreath, reputedly the last native Cornish speaking person in the land, was a native here and her memorial stands in the churchyard. In this photo can clearly be seen the granite coffin rests and also the Celtic 'Cornish' cross built into the churchyard wall.

Above: A beautiful slide, taken by Gibson of Penzance *c.* 1900. It is looking down over Mousehole harbour and illustrates the way the town has built up around the harbour. Mousehole was sacked by the Spaniards during their raid on Mounts Bay in 1595.

Below: A much later slide showing the harbour at low water. A proliferation of small boats are clustered under the sturdily-built harbour walls; a few traditional clinker-built punts are moored along the beach. The crane to the right of the harbour entrance was used to lift and place bulks of timber across the quay gaps to protect the vessels in the harbour from waves during gales.

Left: An evocative image of the Keigwin Arms, Mousehole. This medieval house with its granite pillars is now a private residence and at the time of this photograph was a public house. This house survived the Spanish raid of 1595 and was at one time known as the Spaniards House.

Below: Mousehole looking from Gurnick Street back towards the old quay. The quay wall is being used as a washing line for drying sails and barked drift-nets hang drying from every available point. These were probably barked in Tregenza's bark house in Duck Street. Sights like this are long gone.

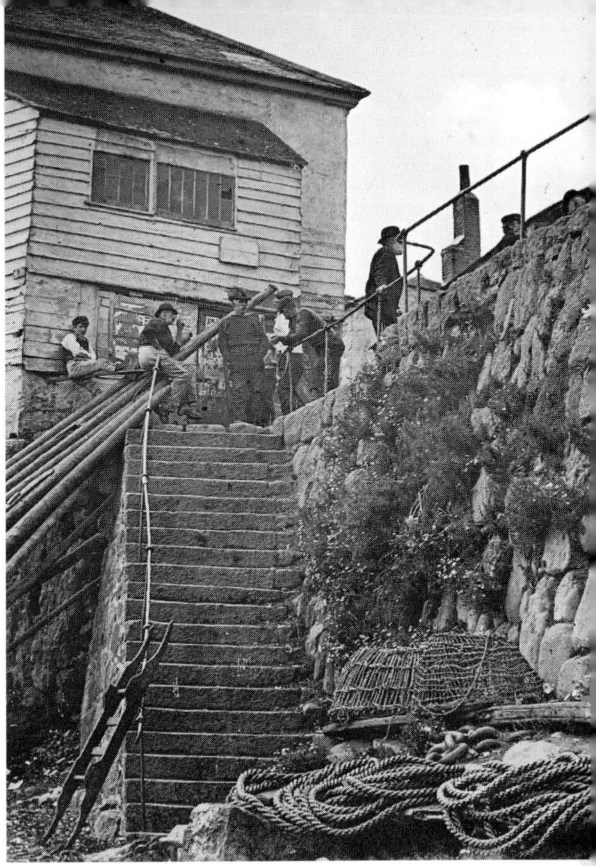

Right: Mousehole, the steps leading from the beach up to the road, the cellars and the Ship Inn. At the bottom of the steps is a hand-barrow leaning against the railings, coils of rope on a chain and a couple of old inkwell withy pots. At the top of the steps are a group of fishermen enjoying a yarn. The building at the top of these steps can again be seen in the centre of the next photo, just past the Ship Inn.

Below: What atmosphere this photograph of Mousehole has; the building on the right is the present day Ship Inn. When this photo was taken the part of the building in the foreground was Rowe's bakery, the far end is the Ship Inn. On the railings are nets that have been barked. The fishing fleet are moored to chains on the water's edge, and a pilchard seine boat is laid up on the slip.

Above: A wonderful slide showing how busy the little harbour of Mousehole was at the turn of the twentieth century. Behind the boat-crammed harbour barked nets can be seen on the railings. Behind the harbour scene is Raginnis Hill which leads up to the road to Lamorna. The row of cottages under Raginnis Hill on the left is called The Cliff.

Below: Looking back at Mousehole harbour. In the foreground, by an empty maun, a couple sit on an upturned punt. In the background sails dry on the harbour wall and barked nets adorn the railings all the way along The Cliff, the row of cottages along the harbour front.

A medieval slipway snakes its way down into Newlyn's medieval quay and two carts awaiting loads are pushed to one side beside an old store. The white cottage on the corner and its neighbours around the corner in the Narrows are now demolished.

Fisherman "Necky" Nowell and his wife lived in one of the cottages in the Narrows. I knew his sons Steven and Michael very well from their visits into Padstow on their fleet of beam trawlers during the Trevose season, which occurs between April and January each year when the dover soles migrate to the Padstow and Trevose Head fishing grounds. Michael's son is Jack Nowell of England RFU fame and we, the Cornish, are all very proud of him and wish him well with his career. At the top of the slip on Upper Strand a group of fishermen stand overlooking Newlyn's original medieval harbour. In the background a group of fishermen lean on the railings outside the Fisherman's Rest, which was a type of Mission where the fishermen could meet.

Above: In this slide of Newlyn we see the Narrows taken from the Mousehole side of Cliff Road, looking towards Penzance. The street on the left before entering the Narrows is Church Street. This little street is now one-way, outward bound to Mousehole. Before the one-way system was introduced this was a notorious bottleneck with hardly room for a horse and cart and a bike to pass!

Below: The Fisherman's Rest at the bottom of Church Street Newlyn. These railings must have seen a multitude of elbows over the decades. The Fisherman's Rest was just that, a place to go and play cards chew the fat or just sit and chill out. On the left hand side adjacent to the Fisherman's Rest is Boase Street.

Above: Strickland Cottages Newlyn taken in the area known as Fradgan, with the old slipway on the left by the cottages. This area has changed considerably since the harbour and fish Market were built on the seaward side of the cottages.

Below: A lovely photo of the roughly-cobbled Bowjey in Newlyn. Children sit in the shade and the washing is out drying. Apparently many of the old cottages were demolished in slum clearance and the area is now covered by a block of flats.

Above: The Cliff Newlyn, opposite the Fisherman's Arms. This is where the fishermen used to congregate for a yarn, have a smoke, spit a bit of baccy and generally put the world to rights. On the left hand side you can see the entrance to the Narrows. What a great view they had along the front although they probably didn't appreciate it.

Left: This slide simply titled 'Newlyn' shows a man dressed in leather thigh boots and sailcloth apron using his Cornish shovel to move pilchards from the brine tanks at the pilchard works in the Strand. The pilchards were shipped every year in barrels to Genoa, Italy. Newlyn had a big pilchard fishery and from the brine tanks they would be packed in barrels in a circle, tail to the outside and nose to the centre, in layers.

Above: The old harbour front buildings along Newlyn's foreshore. The slip is a continuation of Fore Street down onto the Strand and the higher half has upturned punts pulled up out of the water. When the tide was in the road was impassable by foot. The tall building next to Paul sail maker was a pilchard cellar.

Right: This slide of Elizabeth Lanyon was taken by Graystone Birch, one the United Kingdom's finest Victorian photographers. Elizabeth Lanyon was a famous Newlyn fishwife carrying her wicker creel on her back, the weight being transferred by a strap across her forehead; this was used to carry fish or shellfish. A face full of character, attired in her bonnet and traditional dress, she must have been a photographers dream. Elizabeth, known as Betsy, was born Elizabeth Leah. In 1832 she married a fisherman called Francis Lanyon at Paul church. She was buried on 6 July 1892 aged eighty-six. She was a great favourite with the Newlyn school of artists featuring in several paintings, the most famous being *Among the missing* where she is in the front leading away the young woman. Walter Langley also painted her portrait.

A slightly later view of Newlyn harbour with the Fisherman's Arms far left taken from the Strand, looking back into the old quay.

Looking down at Newlyn's medieval harbour through Trewarveneth Street. Higher up the street out of the photo is the Old Manor House, the best example of an early seventeenth century merchant's house in Newlyn. The town was sacked in 1595 by the Spanish and many properties were rebuilt after this date being funded by the prosperity of the thriving fishing industry.

Above: On the foreshore at Newlyn. In the foreground fishermen and women unload the day's catch into waiting carts; behind the carts are empty mauns and a hand-barrow strewn on the rocks. Behind the workers one can see along the seafront past Wherrytown mine buildings, Bolitho Gardens and the slipway where Peake's boats were launched. Further along to the right is the old road which was still in situ when this was taken. St Mary's Church in Chapel Street, Penzance is in the background.

Right: A very interesting photo of the tub race during Penzance regatta in 1903. What a dangerous-looking sport and so far off the harbour, the vessels look, to say the least, unstable and uncontrollable—it must have been a race of great hilarity. In the background is the foreshore and Abbey Slip, behind them the original St Mary's Church.

Above: An Edwardian view of Penzance promenade, locally known as 'The Landings' which used to run across the prom to the Wherrytown end. Sue a local reminisced 'It was great for swimming off at high tide. Nice deep water to dive into and you could hire deckchairs on the prom in those days. Good for swimming after band nights at the Wints!'

Left: The Land's End Walk 26 May 1904. An enthusiastic crowd follow an exhausted Mr Ford as he wins the race from Penzance to Land's End and back again. It was called the Land's End walk despite it finishing in Penzance.

Above: Great patriotic celebrations outside St John's Hall Penzance on Mafeking Day. The papers report there was a great spontaneous celebration when news of Mafeking being relieved was received in May 1900. Everyone took to the streets and flags were waved and bugles blown, a real party atmosphere.

Below: The Penzance lifeboat pictured on its carriage, being pulled from the lifeboat house along the Quay, past Quay Street with St Mary's Church in the background. Pulled by a team of heavy horses, some of the crew are on board wearing their cork lifejackets and oilers ready for the launch.

A charming Victorian view of a bustling and thriving Market Jew Street, Penzance. Symond's Chemist shop is far left, the imposing building in the centre of the image is the Market House. Humphrey Davey's imposing statue was installed in front of it in1872. A proliferation of horse drawn vehicles litter the street along with evidence of the horses passing by, the sacks in one of the carts are all dated 1885.

This crystal-sharp slide by Gibson of Penzance is a view looking back towards the town and Mount's Bay from the Barracks at Chyandour. The large building in the foreground was part of the old police station. The road bottom left is Chyandour Cliff. To the right and behind the harbour is St Mary's Church, by the sea to the far right of the photo is the distinctive dome of the Market House; the present day Lloyds Bank. To the left of the bank running down towards the harbour is the main shopping street called Market Jew Street; the very large building below left is the railway station.

Cornwall's most iconic sight, St Michael's Mount in Mounts Bay *c.* 1900. St Michael's Mount is an island joined to the mainland at Marazion by a causeway of granite sets, at high tide the mount is only accessible by boat. The castle and chapel have been home to the St Aubyn family since 1650, but the building dates back much further with some parts dating from the twelfth century. The harbour is fifteenth century and between the Mount and harbour is a small village for the estate workers.

A slide *c.* 1900 looking out from St Michael's Mount Battery back over the gatehouse, village and fifteenth-century harbour towards the causeway which can be seen snaking towards Marizion across Mounts Bay.

The SS *Tripolitania* on Loe Bar near Helston; she was an Italian steel steam cargo ship built in 1897. She met her fate on Boxing day 1912 in a severe south-westerly gale. She sat upright and undamaged on the sand-bar and great effort was put in to digging her out; tugs were standing by to pull her off, but her fate was sealed when the weather turned and they had to run for shelter. She was eventually sold for scrap.

Above and below: These two slides are of the chocolate box fishing village of Church Cove on the Lizard peninsula; quaint old thatched cottages as the top photo illustrates interact with the fishermen's more solid and practical buildings such as these cellars in the bottom photo. The fishermen pull their boats up the beach using a winch to keep them safe from the ravages of the sea.

Left: Here is an example of a privately taken slide *c.* 1940, where people would record their holidays and give slide shows locally on their return home. In this slide three of the holiday party pose on the wall and behind them is the imposing Lloyds signal station at Porthcurnow on the Lizard. This is where Marconi conducted his wireless communication tests in 1901.

Below: The courtyard of Godolphin House at Godolphin Cross near Helston, a fifteenth century manor house owned and lived in by the Godolphin family until the middle of the eighteenth century. Much of the original house was demolished in 1805 and the house turned into a farmhouse. This house is steeped in history and has been owned by the National trust since 2007.

Bass point the Lizard 1913. The sad sight of the steel-hulled 271 foot-long three-masted fully-rigged *Cromdale*; she was the last ship built for the Australian wool trade, built in 1891 by Barclay Curie & Co. Glasgow for Donald Rose & Co. of Aberdeen. Even wrecked she is a magnificent sight with her sails out and rigging flapping. Thankfully no lives were lost.

St Ruan's holy well or Grade Well, stands alone in a small roadside meadow. The well house is a small square fourteenth-century granite building measuring only five feet square and six feet high. In the photo you can see inside the well house itself and two of the three small ledges for seating around the well. The well, dedicated to St Ruan, still has clear water flowing from it.

Above: Looking north from above the harbour over the quaint village of Cadgwith. This slide dating from around the early 1900s clearly shows the thatched roofs of most of the cottages. Behind the dwelling houses on the hillside are small walled strips of land which would be used by cottagers to grow vegetables.

Below: A chocolate box photo of a row of cottages in Cadgwith. This idyllic image makes one forget the hardships the inhabitants would have had to endure putting food on the plates on such a barren and inhospitable piece of coast.

This charming photo *c.* 1940 looking north-west from above the beach shows the cluttered strand area of the harbour. Withy pots litter the scene, barked nets on a gig, a herring boat has been pulled up on the slip—not an engine or motor powered boat in sight.

Cadgwith harbour looking back towards the village in the 1950s. All the boats are neatly pulled up onto the beach. This fishing harbour traditionally used cove boats but in these modern times the commercial boats working from the cove tend to be slightly larger. A tractor is used to move them in an out of the water rather than the old winch which use to be used to pull them up the beach.

Another charming image of Cadgwith, this time looking out to sea and down past the old thatched cottages in Barn Hill.

The backstreets of St Kevern, looking across the village square towards the parish church which is dedicated to St Akeveranus. The church is now peculiar for having a peel of ten bells, though at the time of this photo the church only had a peel of eight bells. St Kevern is famous as the start of the Cornish rebellion of 1497 led by local blacksmith Michael An Gof, a statue of him stands in the village.

Above: Surprisingly there are almost as many cars as punts on this short stretch of foreshore at Helford Passage in this 1940s slide. A pedestrian ferry works daily from here across to Helford.

Below: Helford village on the banks of the Helford River. In ancient times this little village was a very important port before being superseded by Gweek. The ferry from Helford Passage plies its trade across to this charming village.

Above: An Edwardian slide of Manaccan which is within Mannacan parish on the Lizard Peninsula, it is in an area known as Meneage. The area is steeped in history, only recently Boden Vean fogue was rediscovered by a local farmer. Manaccan can also boast of having had a Celtic monastery.

Porthoustock looking down on the shingle beach, a few of the local boats that worked from the harbour are pulled up onto the safety of the beach. This slide taken in 1932 shows the chocolate box thatched cottages clustered around the beach.

Opposite below: Coverack village and beach located on the Lizard Peninsula.

Above and Left: Two Edwardian slides of Constantine Churchtown. The top slide is looking towards the parish church which is dedicated to the sixth century Saint, St Constantine, a village feast is still celebrated in his name on or around the 9 March. The bottom slide is of Church Square.

Port Navas at the head of Port Navas Creek; it is a charming little village on the Helford River near Mawnan Smith.

A view from the Inner Harbour looking across from Bar Terrace towards the Custom House Quay and the town of Falmouth. The large shed in the front is the railway's goods sheds with the railway cottages on the left. Behind the goods sheds was the timber pond and here wood was soaked with salt water for use later in the boatyards. The small wall seen just above the goods sheds enclosed the mill pond; the derelict building standing on it was a tide mill which had ceased to operate in 1862. The warehouses behind that belonged to Harvey's timber yard and the shipyards of Symonds & Burt. The striped funnel of a Dockyard tug is probably in front of Submarine Quay and can be seen just below Customs House Quay. In the distance it looks like they are building the container for the gas works.

Fish Strand Quay; its name reflects what it was used for as this was where the fish were landed for market. Originally the catch was landed on a beach but a short pier was built about 1790 and then enlarged in 1871 to give boats easier access.

Falmouth: Customs House Quay, the quay was originally called the Town Quay; it was renamed when the Customs House moved here in 1790. The quay was built about 1670 by Sir Peter Killigrew. The Royal Mail began their Packet Ship service from here in 1688 and sent mail all around the world until the age of steam arrived in the 1850s. Next door to the Globe Hotel was the harbour master's house.

Above: Lower Castle Road, St Mawes, in the 1940s. St Mawes is a small town opposite Falmouth and accessible by taking a one-mile ferry crossing on the Place Ferry across the River Fal. St Mawes is famous for its sixteenth century castle built by Henry VII to protect the river.

Below: Ferry Quay at Feock; the King Harry Ferry runs from this quay across to Philleigh. The ferry has been running for many centuries being named after King Henry and there is a conflict of opinion as to whether it was Henry VI or Henry VII. This ferry was voted the most beautiful ferry crossing in the world.

A beautiful slide showing a man in his punt on Truro River looking towards the Cathedral before it had a tower. The cathedral's foundation stone was laid on 20 May 1880 by the Duke of Cornwall later to become Edward VII. The central tower which is not evident in this photo was built in 1905, helping to date this image.

This slide is a view looking up St Mary's Street towards Truro Cathedral pre-1905. The part of the cathedral in the front of the photo is part of the sixteenth century St Mary's Parish Church which was cleverly incorporated into the Victorian building.

Above: St Clement, a small village in the Tresillian Valley south east of Truro. This chocolate box image shows a thatched cottage in the foreground, with the parish church in the background.

Below: St Anthony's Lighthouse stands on St Anthony's Head on the eastern side of the entrance to Falmouth Harbour. The lighthouse was built by Olver of Falmouth for Trinity House in 1835; amazingly the light was not powered by electricity until 1954. The bell that can be seen hanging from the gallery on the front of the lighthouse was replaced with a fog-horn in 1954 and donated to a local church where it sat on the lawn for many years until sadly it was melted down.

A beautiful image of the hamlet of Percuil in the early 1900s, much of the surrounding countryside now is owned by the National Trust and it is now designated as an AONB – an Area of Outstanding Natural Beauty.

Porthscatho harbour. Porthscatho is a small coastal village on the Roseland Peninsula. At the bottom of the steps are withy inkwell pots strewn about and nets are drying on the railings. Obviously at this time this photo was taken it was a busy little south coast harbour.

Right: Portloe harbour slipway. Portloe is a beautiful little fishing village in Veryan parish on the Roseland Peninsula. Portloe was the childhood home of my gramfer Bob Johns, his family trace back in Portloe to Seraphim Johns who was born in the seventeenth century.

Below: Portmellon a small village one mile south of Mevagissey is famous for its boat building firm of Gary Mitchell, who built many fine wooden boats. These boasted incredible lines and included many racing yachts which were launched over the harbour wall down temporary slipways, after being manhandled from the yard down the street against all odds.

Above: An early panoramic image of Mevagissey harbour *c.*1900. Barked nets are drying on the harbour walls as a fishing vessel departs on a mill-pond-flat sea.

Below: A fantastic slide of East Quay Mevagissey at high tide in the very early 1900s. The reflections of the moored fishing fleet are a wonderful sight.

Above: Mevagissey harbour looking in the opposite direction. It appears to have been taken on the same day by the same photographer as the previous image. The sailing fishing vessels neatly moored inside Victoria Pier on a beautiful evening showing this charming port off at its best. This is how most people visualise a Cornish fishing port.

Below: A family enjoy relaxing on the beach in Mevagissey harbour in the 1950s.

An old Mevagissey fisherman sitting on the rocks examines his withy inkwell pot looking closely for damage to repair; a few broken withies in need of attention are evident near the bottom of the pot.

This photo taken in the 1930s shows doors in the roof at the Cliff, Mevagissey. Note the graffiti on the wall, not like the tags of today but carefully drawn sailing vessels.

Above: Trelissick Manor farm near St Austell. This farmhouse has hardly changed on the outside since this slide was taken around 1910; it is now used for farm holidays.

Below: Roche Rock and hermitage situated on the moors beside the road just outside of the village to which it give its name. The hermitage of St Conan later became a chapel dedicated in 1409 to Saint Michael. Access to the Chapel or hermitage is via a rusty ladder affixed to the rocks. There is speculation that this site could well have been used for pagan ceremonies for thousands of years.

Lostwithiel's medieval Bridge looking towards St Bartholomew's Church whose tower can be seen in the background. Lostwithiel was in medieval times the capital of the Duchy of Cornwall and this bridge dates from that time, it is now rightly a scheduled ancient monument.

A charming Edwardian view of the Parade at Lostwithiel; the medieval bridge can be seen in the background.

Above: This slide was taken from outside of the Royal Oak looking down Duke Street across Liddicoat Road and further on down North Street. In this photo the first house on the right hand side of Duke Street is Duke House.

Below: A rare view of a street hawker with his barrow full of chestnuts, taken in North Street Lostwithiel *c.* 1930. A hard but honest way to earn a living!

Above: The platform of Lostwithiel station looking back over the town with the distinctive St Bartholomew's church clearly visible in the background. The station escaped Dr Beeching's cuts and trains run every two hours towards Plymouth and Penzance and through trains go onwards to Paddington.

Below: A horse and over-full wagon are trudging up towards the thirteenth century gateway of Restormal Castle Lostwithiel. The castle is now owned by English Heritage.

Above: This Arial photo of Restormal Castle illustrates perfectly the circular bailey built in the thirteenth century on top of the Norman motte. The castle was in constant use up until the civil war; it only experienced action once during its long history that was during the Civil War when the Parliamentarians were ousted by Charles the First's forces. After the Civil War the castle fell into disrepair. The castle stands on the high ground overlooking the River Fowey.

Below: A slide of a backstreet in Lerryn village taken in the 1940s. Lerryn is a small village on the River Lerryn which is a tributary of the river Fowey.

Another image from the 1940s, here we are looking from the west river bank of the River Fowey at Golant looking up the hill towards the New Inn on the right.

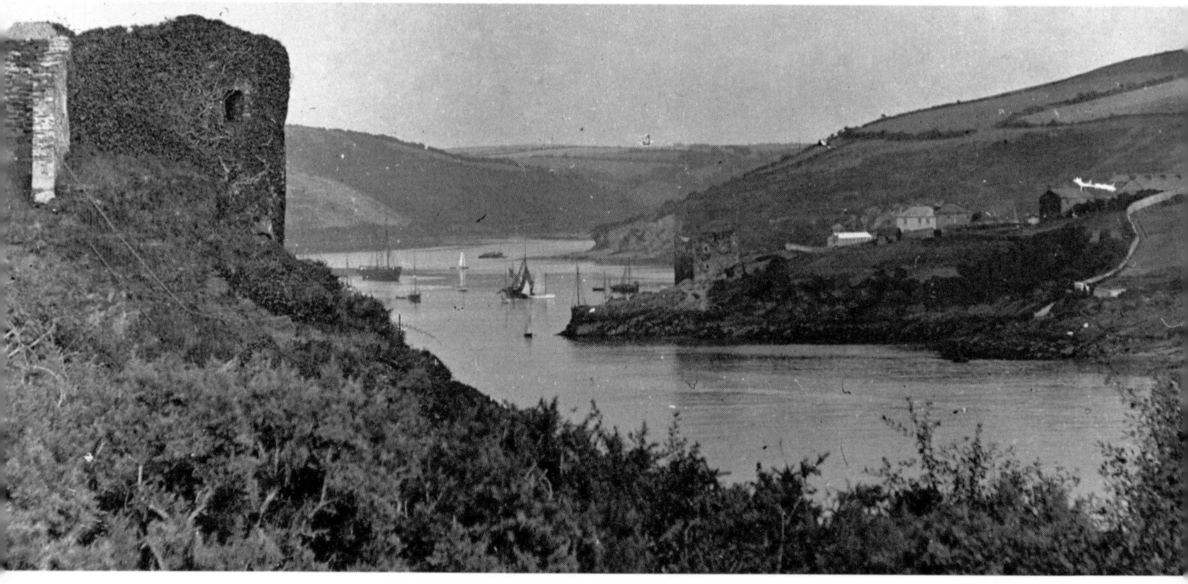

Looking up the river Fowey from St Catherine's Point. Poluan is visible on the opposite side of the river. The ruins of a small castle can be seen in the foreground, on the Polruan side of the river can be seen the remains of the blockhouse which was built in 1380, along with another blockhouse on the Fowey side between which ran a chain along the river bed which could be raised to defend the mouth of the river against attack.

A photo taken in the early years of the twentieth century looking from Polruan Quay across the Fowey River west towards Fowey, which is seen in the background sprawling along the river bank.

A fantastic photo of the Bodinnick horse ferry; the china clay wharfs in the background are littered with steamers. This ancient ferry still runs to this day from Fowey to Bodinnick.

Old cottages at Bodinnick near Fowey, the four boys don't look very happy at being asked to pose for this charming photo.

Blue Cottage in Bodinnick has had a very interesting past, as the bars on the cellar window at the foot of the steps suggest, it was once used as a jail. It held prisoners brought from Fowey before being sent to Launceston for the assizes.

Right: Bodinnick, looking down past Blue Cottage situated on the right with the dog on the steps, down past Ye Old Ferry House to the banks of the River Fowey and the town of Fowey on the opposite bank.

Below: Looking back down the bustling Fowey River over the laid up steam ships towards Polruan, the Blockhouse mentioned earlier is clearly visible on the point.

An old fisherman enjoying a rest on the footpath to the south of Polperro. He is wearing his traditional knit frock and the old style of beard that runs under the chin, but clean shaven on the face. Despite his obvious age he looks physically very fit and strong—a testament to hard work.

Above and below: Two slides of the ketch *Two Sisters* anchored outside of Polperro Harbour.

A beautiful Victorian image of the fishing fleet. Polperro Gaffers are moored in Polperro's outer harbour looking back over the town.

Opposite above: Taken from a slightly lower angle, this is another view looking back into Polperro harbour past the moored fishing fleet.

Opposite below: Polperro 1931, the *Lily* FY 302 having pots and backs put aboard at the beginning of the season ready to take to sea for shooting. *Lily* was built by Ferris of Looe in the 1890s. She was owned by Curtis of Polperro until 1931 when she was sold to Mr Peter Pye who had her fitted out as a cruising yacht. He sailed her all over the world, and wrote several books about his adventures. She is still afloat and cruising with her present owner Robert Chudleigh under the name of *Moonraker.*

FY302
LILY + FOWEY

Above: The Pier Polperro looking from left to right Willy Wilcock's cottage; Charlie Wilcock's cottage; Fisherman's House and Pierin House.

Left: A shipwright is working with his adze on the pier at Polperro. This photo was taken in 1931, not that long ago but yet a fishing port with only sail-powered vessels in evidence. This original slide is one half of a very small glass stereoscopic slide, this image measuring no more than 1 inch square.

Above: Polperro's inner harbour at low tide, looking past the moored fishing fleet, this quaint little harbour has changed little over the last one hundred and ten years since this photo was taken.

Below: Another idyllic view of the timeless Polperro harbour; a fisherman sculls past the laid up fishing fleet *c*. 1920.

Fishing lugger FY 200 moored in Polperro Harbour; she has her legs attached to keep her upright when the tide ebbs and she dries out.

Polperro harbour taken at low tide, this slide is amazingly crisp and clear a credit to the photographer's art.

Above: Tide's out in Polperro, but fishing vessel *Honorary* sits quite comfortably on her detachable legs.

Below: Looking back into Polperro harbour at low tide in the 1940s.

Above: Lansallos Street looking towards Polperro harbour, an old fisherman in his traditional knit frock walks his dog up the street.

Right: A Polperro fisherman mends his driftnets on the quayside while two mystified young girls look on in cross-legged wonderment.

In one of Polperro's backstreets, a female hawker is offering a pair of shoes for sale; these are sights of the not-so-distant past which are unlikely to return in this day and age.

Two girls skip over the Saxon Bridge past Couch's House named after the naturalist Jonathan Couch who lived in the house in the nineteenth century. The house dates from 1595 and at the time this photo was taken it was a Museum and Art Gallery.

A cottage in Polperro's main street, many of the cottages have steps to the first floor living accommodation leaving the ground floors free to be cellars for storing fishing gear.

The River Pol runs through the little village of Polperro past the backs of houses, a Saxon bridge still survives and the river still runs under it, eventually emerging into the harbour.

Another photo of Polperro's backstreets, how closely packed the houses are, and evidence of flying freehold abounds everywhere. How cramped conditions were for couples with in some cases very large families.

The Warren Polperro, it is not difficult to see why this area got its name, again narrow cobbled streets as is normal for Polperro's back streets.

An old lady in the Warren Polperro carrying a pail. It is interesting to see the design, the pail tapers in from the bottom making it less inclined to slop and spill.

A Polperro fisherman is pictured carrying two withy pots walking down to the harbour along the Warren.

Looks like washing day half way down West Looe Hill. This photo is looking across the town towards East Looe in the distance from West Looe Hill.

The Jolly Sailor, West Looe, probably the oldest pub in Looe and one of the oldest in the country being built in 1516. Inside it still has retained its old-world charm.

Right: This photo has been scanned from one half of a tiny stereoscopic lantern slide and it shows Fore Street, Looe in 1931. It is amazing how the detail has come up from an image no more than 1 inch square.

Below: A Looe fishermen stands outside of Cobblers Cottage at the bottom of West Looe Hill, by the junction of Princes Square and Fore Street. The little drang or alleyway beside the cottage led to a court behind the slated house where a dairy was situated, it looks like two milk cans are on a ledge on the wall. A quaint little one up one down cottage but I know from my gran's similar cottage in Padstow that small cottages such as this were difficult to live in with no toilet, a shared toilet in the back court was normal.

The *Emma* and some of the Looe fishing fleet are moored up in East Looe below Looe Bridge.

West Looe quayside, looking up river towards Looe Bridge.

This slide is taken from Wooldown in East Looe looking across at West Looe. On East Looe quayside can be seen the wooden frames and overhead crane which were used to lift granite into boats waiting on the quay side, this image dates from *c.* 1895.

Taken *c.* 1895 this slide is looking up river from Hannafore Lane, West Looe towards East Looe. On the seafront can be seen a large square building with an inner courtyard, this was called the Albatross and was used for curing and packing fish. Sadly it was demolished in the 1960s and is the site of the present day lifeboat station.

This photo (*c*. 1895) is of the entrance to Looe from the sea is taken from the Downs West Looe, looking across at East Looe.

Lower Street East Looe, a cobbled backstreet behind what used to be the old library.

A young lad is carrying two substantial wicker baskets and a milk pail along Church Street, East Looe *c*. 1910.

Above: East Looe's quayside, a couple of fishermen talk fishy tales.

Below: Fishermen at East Looe fleet their nets onto their fishing boat.

Above: This photograph is taken from Little Pier in East Looe looking across at West Looe; this is very popular spot for photographers.

Left: The old guildhall in East Looe, this fifteenth century building—now a museum—was the merchant's guildhall in early days, it also houses cells from when it was used as a jail when Magistrates' Sessions were held. The building now houses the town museum and is well worth a visit to enjoy both this ancient building and the Museum's interesting exhibits.

This slide *c.* 1940 is a view of Lower Market Street, East Looe, looking towards Buller Street.

Old cottages weave their way along a higgledy-piggledy Middle Market Street, East Looe. Streets like this give Looe its distinctive charm and character.

Above: This is a slide of the East Looe valley, the road carries on up the hill to the village of Trewidland.

Below: A photograph of St Keynes Well taken about 1910. The well of dressed granite was built in the sixteenth century and rebuilt in the 1930s when the road was widened. A holy well the water from which is made famous by the former poet laureate Robert Southern, a stanza about the well goes: 'The quality that man or wife whom chance or choice attains first of this sacred spring to drink thereby the mastery gains.'

Right: The Pipe Well Liskeard dating from the fourteenth century is dedicated to St Martin. The well is fed by four springs and has never run dry, its waters are supposed to possess magical properties curing blindness.

Below: St Stephen's Hill on Thomas Road leading up to Launceston Castle in the distance.

Above: Sadly no longer standing, these quaint old buildings were at the top of Northgate Street just below the church, and were demolished in the 1960s during the slum clearance despite strong opposition from local residents. The buildings that replaced this bustling historic medieval street are soulless and uninspiring. Progress is not always a good thing.

Below: In the foreground are the ruins of the twelfth-century Augustinian Launceston Priory, with Launceston Castle dominating the back ground. The priory was built on this site in Newport Launceston beside the river Kensey in 1155.The priory was a massive and impressive building but demolished following King Henry VIII's dissolution of the monasteries.

Above: This ancient packhorse bridge is called Priors Bridge; it spans the river at Kensey, adjacent to the Augustinian priory in Newport Launceston.

Right: Southgate Arch, Launceston, this is the only remaining gate into the city from the original medieval walled town. Launceston was the only walled town in Cornwall. The gatehouse would have had a portcullis, drawbridge and moat. In the sixteenth century the buildings in this photo replaced the original fortified buildings to make them more suitable for use as a residence. During the early nineteenth century the building was used as the town jail, it ceased use as a jail in 1884.

Above: Calstock. Looking up the valley towards Gunnislake.

Below: Wier Head Calstock, the left hand side of the river is the Cornish side showing the industrial buildings, which are the brickworks below Gunnislake and were known as Bealeswood. The works fronted the river and bricks were loaded onto barges from a small quay. Between 1870 and 1900 Calstock and the surrounding area produced more building bricks than any other centre west of Lee Moor. Thomas Westlake took over the Gunnislake Bealeswood works; he also owned another at Calstock. The brick making industry continued in and around Calstock and Gunnislake until the 1930s when the trade was killed by the growing of the cement block industry.

Above: Lady Emma's Cottage on the Mount Edgecombe Estate on the banks of the river Tamer; at this time it appears to be a very busy tea rooms.

Below: The Meadow Cawsand. This lovely meadow has unfortunately been turned into the Cawsand car park.

Above: This is a most curious slide of an artist's impression of Saltash YMCA and it states in the cartouche L. Leighton Fouracre Architect ARIBA Archt. Oct. 1906. The building was located in Fore Street and was converted into the Saltash Working Men's Club and later demolished.

Below: On the banks of the River Tamar under the Cornish side of Isambard Kingdom Brunel's famous Royal Albert Bridge lays the town of Saltash, here you can see Saltash's old harbour side buildings along the beach with the railway running through and above the quaint Cornish town.

Above: An atmospheric slide of Albert Road, locally known as Station Hill as it lies beside the railway station, looking down the hill towards the River Tamar and along the Royal Albert Bridge. Under the bridge on the Devon side of the river can be seen St Budeaux. Here the yard where the spans of the bridge were made was located in the early 1850s.

Below: Mining china clay at Bugle, china clay or kaolin is extracted from granite that has started to decompose; kaolin the geological name for china clay is extracted using high pressure hoses called monitors, the sludge is washed out of the cliffs and runs down to the bottom into a sump, from where it is pumped to settling tanks. The pump engine house can be seen top centre of picture.

Above: The linhay at Goonbarrow. Linhays were huge sheds with open sides where the cakes of clay were dried. The cakes can clearly be seen stacked up and the chimneys at the far end of the building for the furnace which would be lit to produce warm air to dry the cakes.

Below: Cornwall, apart from geologically being made of granite outcrops, has substantial amounts of slate from the Devonian period which are rich in marine fossils. At Delabole the slate is particularly dense and splits very well making it a first class roofing material. Slate has been mined at this quarry continuously since the fifteenth century making it the oldest quarry in England still in use. At one time it was the deepest man-made pit in the world, though it has since been superseded by overseas quarries. At the time this photograph was taken 500 men were employed in the quarry.

Botallack Mine, Crowans, St Just. This dramatic mine perched on the cliffs of West Penwith is now owned by the National Trust and is no longer working. It had a myriad of levels and tunnels, its workings extending 400 metres out under the Atlantic Ocean to a depth of 250 fathoms. Adjacent to the tin mine are two arsenic refining works, the mines had calciners. Calciners are roasting furnaces used to remove arsenic from the partially concentrated tin ore. In the early twentieth century, along with the labyrinth of stone chambers used to collect the arsenic trioxide which was oxidised from the arsenic sulphides in the ore, during the roasting process as the fumes from the calciner passed through the tunnels condensing the fumes back into a solid. This was part of the tin concentration process as the arsenic had to be removed before the final concentration; a tin concentrate containing arsenic would be unsalable as the arsenic could not be removed in the smelting process and arsenic in the tin metal made it hard and unworkable. Botallack had no arsenic refinery it simply sold on the crude to a specialist arsenic refining company.

An incredible slide of Levant copper mine taken about 1890. The photograph shows the beam winding engine, pumping house and headgear on the edge of the cliff. The mine opened in 1820 although it probably was working earlier than that, and closed one hundred and ten years later. Levant mine like Botallack stretched under the sea, but Levant tunnelled two and a half kilometres out under the Atlantic Ocean to a depth of 600 metres. The mine is now famous for having the only Cornish beam engine in a mine anywhere in the world still in steam and on its original site. Spare a thought for the photographer scrambling down the cliff with all his equipment to take this historic shot. This slide was probably taken from the path that led down to the adit that was driven into the mine from the bottom of the Zawn just above sea level.

A wonderful slide of the pumping engine used to pump water out of Watson's Shaft, Prince of Wales Copper Mine. This photo was taken in the very early 1900s. Watson's Shaft was the main shaft in the mine. Twenty years or more ago all the buildings were easily accessible and photographable. Regrettably, this is no longer the case. The mine was briefly reworked in the early twentieth century and closed just before the First World War. During its main period of working, from 1864 to 1892, the mine first produced mainly copper ore, though yielded significant quantities of tin as it grew deeper, stamps and tin dressing floors being put in 1888. Arsenic and iron pyrites were also produced as by-products. The rare type of hollow work, or trellis construction of the engine beam, or bob can clearly be seen in the photo, and the big bell on top of the engine house served as a timekeeper.

The tin and copper miners at the Prince of Wales mine *c.* 1900 pose for a photograph before going below grass. Note the lumps of sticky clay, which was sourced in the St Agnes area, on the felt miners' helmets. The clay was used to hold their candles in place. These were hard men used to physical work in very difficult and hot conditions. The man in the top row far right with a cap and beard is William Thomas.

Opposite: The pumping engine at Wheal Kitty St Agnes used to pump water out of Sara's Shaft. Wheal Kitty was opened in the 1830s and it was mined to a depth of 180 fathoms. This was the main shaft of the mine when it restarted in the twentieth century. Wheal Kitty was worked mainly for tin although a small amount of copper was sold out of the mine. The mine worked on and off until 1930 when she finally closed. The sixty-five inch Perran Foundry beam engine made in 1852 was housed in this pumping house from 1910. At the time this photo was taken the mine would have employed about 220 people.

Above: This slide may be a copy of an earlier photograph, the only reason I think this is because the original photo must have been taken during the 1860s when this mine in the Redruth area was working. Left to right are the beam winder engine house and stack, the hand capstan and the 70-inch pumping engine. The high capstan shears were said to have been the tallest ever erected in Cornwall. The mine had its main workings on the north side of the steep Sparnon Hill, on the southern side of Redruth town, later it was part of Pedn-an-drea mine which was a little further north. St Andrew's Church constructed in 1883–1884 is on the site of the mine just south of the rising ground of the present day Heaton Terrace.

This photograph when first I discovered it caused great excitement, as prior to William Thomas's box of slides coming to light only a couple of photographs of women going underground in Cornwall had been known. These ladies at King Edward Mine I believe to be three of the four daughters of William Thomas Head of Mining at Camborne School of Mines and his wife Mary. Left to right are Mary Ethel Thomas or Enid Evelyn Thomas, Mrs Mary Ann Thomas, Miriam Olive Thomas and Christina May Thomas. In the second row the short man third from right, is Head of Mining William Thomas to his right his son Cedric Thomas and next to him his uncle Charles Frederick Thomas, quite a Thomas family group. Note the bundles of candles around their necks. The photograph has been dated to 1903 as the overhead tramway looks reasonably new and has no handrails; the mill came on stream in 1904. In the background is the building which housed the mill engine, this building still exists little changed to this day.

Opposite: This slide *c.* 1900 and most of the other mining slides came from a box of slides belonging to William Thomas who was the Mine Manager and Head of Mining at Camborne School of Mines in the very early twentieth century. The slide is titled 'Welsh and Cornish mine engineers visit to Dolcoath'. The image has appeared in other books with a different caption, this caption is definitely correct being in Thomas's own hand. What a stern looking bunch they were. The men are posed just outside of the house of the new Dolcoath vertical air shaft which was installed in the 1890s on the central part of the mine near New Sump Shaft. The house is still standing though used for other purposes these days.

This wonderful photograph is taken outside the door of the Count House at King Edward Mine c. 1903. Left to right are Christina May Thomas, Miriam Olive Thomas and their father William Thomas with two unidentified men, they all dressed in their underground clothes and helmets, another very rare photo of ladies in their underground clothes before going below grass. It is possible, but not a certainty that this series of photos were taken by William Thomas's friend photographer J. C. Burrow.

Inside the cage that lowered the miners down into King Edward Mine are William Thomas and daughter Olive, one of her sisters is standing behind her alongside their brother Cedric who is looking through the middle of the group. They are ready to descend into the mine, *c.* 1903.

King Edward Mine, Camborne. This photograph by J. C. Burrow shows two men working a pneumatic rock drill made by Climax of Camborne in the forty fathom level or 400 feet from surface. Note the young lad holding the water spray, rock drilling produces a great deal of very fine dust which can cause silicosis, a lung disease that can eventually kill. This mine was owned and run by Camborne School of Mines, Captain William Thomas was Head of Mining the Principal of the school was J. J. Beringer.

This photograph by Hughes is of stoping at the forty fathom level, King Edward Mine. Stoping is extracting the ore from an underground mine, strong rock is not a perquisite as there are various methods of extracting ore from almost any type of rock. This slide was taken in the Great Flat lode which dips at about 30 degrees to the horizontal, most Cornish lodes are steeped, typically dipping at 70 degrees. The open spaces that is left behind is known as a stope.

Above: The Cathedral – a vast cavern on the 60 fathom level at King Edward Mine Camborne, this photo is by Hughes, the man in the foreground is believed to be Kit Bennetts the mine Foreman or Captain.

Below: This photo by J. C. Burrow was taken at the 40 fathom level of King Edward Mine. Two miners are wearing their resin-impregnated felt hats, they are just lighting a fuse using a tallow candle, prior to lighting he or his colleague would have shouted a warning.

Above: This photo shows a team being supervised by the elderly mine captain, who is in the middle surrounded by his student miners as they climb from the 60–50 fathom levels up wooden ladders which are joined together. It looks an uncomfortable angle and must have been an arduous task.

Below: This slide was taken at the Blue Hills Mine which was in the Jericho Valley St Agnes just above Trevellas Porth. It appears that these three miners are using a sledge hammer to put in a prop above the 66 fathom level. The St Agnes lodes tend to be fairly flat as can be seen here.

Another of J. C. Burrow's slides, this photo is of the ascending man engine at Dolcoath. The man engine was a mechanical means of helping the miners to ascend or descend the shaft; note ladders are also in place for the miners to use if they wish. The rod of the man-engine had small platforms every 12 feet along its length, The engine had a 12-foot stroke, and with each engine stroke the miners were lifted 12 feet to pass through square holes in fixed platforms in the shaft, where they stepped off and waited for the next stroke to take them either up or down. As can be seen these man engines were dangerous and they were the cause of a terrible accident at Levant on the 20 October 1919. Over 100 men were in the man engine ascending when a bracket broke and the timbers fell down the shaft taking the platforms with them killing thirty-one men. The metal strap that broke can be seen at the Levant Engine which is open to the public.

Underground Dolcoath 412 fathom level, on the right are two miners pushing a tram and on the left are three miners, one wielding a sledgehammer they are hand drilling blast holes.

Opposite: This image titled the 375 level near New East Shaft, Dolcoath in J. C. Burrow's book printed in 1893 *Mongst Mines and Miners or Underground scenes by flashlight*, but on the slide it is titled hanging tram road 375 fathom level East Dolcoath. What you are looking at is the underneath of the tramway above where miners are working on the 375 fathom level.

A mill or ore-chute at the 412 fathom level Dolcoath Mine. The shaft being so deep, some 2,500 feet or 800 metres, the temperature would have been around 100 degrees Fahrenheit, so hot that the miners worked almost naked. Here you can see them using long handled Cornish shovels to pull the material into the waiting tram waggons.

Above: A very busy scene by J. C. Burrow taken on the 412 fathom level at Dolcoath. Full trams are being pushed in at least two different directions, miners in the foreground break the rocks to manageable size while at back of shot other miners appear to be working with a bucket or kibble which would be used to raise ore to the surface. Tragically shortly after this image was taken the whole area collapsed killing several men and making this part of the mine unworkable.

Below: Another marvellous photo by J. C. Burrow taken in East Pool Mine, in this photo the miners are overhand stoping—i.e. they are mining upwards, looking at the awkward angle they have to strike at, the miner holding the boring tool must have had great faith in his workmates. East Pool Mine has some surface buildings open to the public, its pumping engine is now owned by the National Trust.

Above: J. C. Burrow captures the miners at work on the seventy fathom tram road in East Pool Mine. A miner swings the sledge while the miner on the floor holds a stoping tool or chisel with two hands. The lady sitting down watching far left is J. C. Burrows the photographer's wife, Mary Jane. She was born in Perranuthnoe and J. C. Burrows was at one time in business with Mary Jane's brother photographer James Sandry who worked from Trelewarren Street in Camborne concentrating mainly on portraiture.

Left: A very busy scene again captured by J. C. Burrow 170 fathom level in East Pool Mine, here the men in the foreground are underhand stoping, i.e. working downwards. I marvel at the strength and skill of these men to swing their hammers in tandem in candlelight in such crowded conditions.

Above: The 170 fathom level East Pool mine, again captured by J. C. Burrow, here a miner pushes a tram over the tramway while two other miners precariously stand on the handrail to work above the tramway bridge, despite the Mines and Quarries Act being in force it was still a very dangerous occupation.

Right: In this slide, J. C. Burrow captures the men ascending the mine on three different ladders whilst others are busy pushing a full tram while an empty tram lies on its side clearing the tracks for the full trams on the 180 fathom level in East Pool mine. Considering the equipment and conditions this is a superb image, well structured, planned and lit.

J. C. Burrow captures the miners on the tramway of East Pool having croust, their pasty, jug of tea and water in the little barrels. The miners are eating their traditional pasty out of paper bags as their hands would have been filthy or 'cabby' as we would say in Cornwall.

Another photograph of croust time, farther north in Padstow we know this midmorning meal as crib time. Dialects in Cornwall differ dependant on the parish you are in. These miners are eating their bagged pasties by candlelight. There is a story of a miner called Dunstan from Chacewater; he had a row with his wife Lizzie, she held a bit of a grudge and the next day when he settled down at croust time with his mates and bit into his pasty he found it full of shards of broken cloam or pot to the great hilarity of his fellow miners, After this episode Lizzie was always known as Sherdy Dunstan. On the right you will see a young boy, when boys were strong enough, eleven or twelve years of age they would have gone down the mine and started with easy jobs gradually becoming a miner in a practical apprenticeship.

Another image by J. C. Burrow taken in the 355 fathom level at Cooks Kitchen Mine engine shaft, probably prior to 1895. Miners drilling blast – holes, the man sitting on the platform is holding a steel and the other two are using hammers.

This is a most unusual slide of moving copper ore at a smelting works in Penzance; the only copper smelting works in Penzance was Chyandour which closed in 1912. This is where I believe this photo was taken. There was also a copper smelting works in Newlyn called Trereife that

closed in 1896.The two men are filling a two-handled barrow. These barrows were common just over one hundred years ago but now they are a thing of the past; the last one I have heard of being in use was at Gevor in the 1980s.